Tortoises

By Chuck Miller

Raintree

ANIMALS OF THE RAINFOREST

www.raintreepublishers.co.uk
Visit our website to find out more information about Raintree books.

To order:
☎ Phone 44 (0) 1865 888112
🖷 Send a fax to 44 (0) 1865 314091
💻 Visit the Raintree Bookshop at www.raintreepublishers.co.uk to browse our catalogue and order online.

First published in Great Britain by Raintree Publishers, Halley Court, Jordan Hill, Oxford, OX2 8EJ, part of Harcourt Education.
Raintree is a registered trademark of Harcourt Education Ltd.

Originated by Dot Gradations Ltd
Printed and bound in Hong Kong and China by South China

ISBN 1 844 21105 3
07 06 05 04 03
10 9 8 7 6 5 4 3 2 1

British Library Cataloguing in Publication Data
Miller, Chuck
Tortoises - (Animals of the rainforest)
1. Testudinidae - Juvenile literature
2. Rain forest ecology - Juvenile literature
I.Title 597.9'2
A catalogue for this book is available from the British Library.

Acknowledgements
The publishers would like to thank the following for permission to reproduce photographs:
Root Resources/Kenneth Fink, p, **1**; A.B. Sheldon, pp. **5, 12, 22, 27**; Ben Goldstein; The Roving Tortoise/Tui De Roy, pp. **6, 11, 18, 21, 24, 26, 27–28**; Visuals Unlimited/ Richard Carlton, p. **8**; Ken Lucas, p. **16**.

Cover photograph by Heidi Snell.

Every effort has been made to contact copyright holders of any material reproduced in this book. Any omissions will be rectified in subsequent printings if notice is given to the publishers.

Contents

Any words appearing in the text in bold, **like this**, are explained in the Glossary.

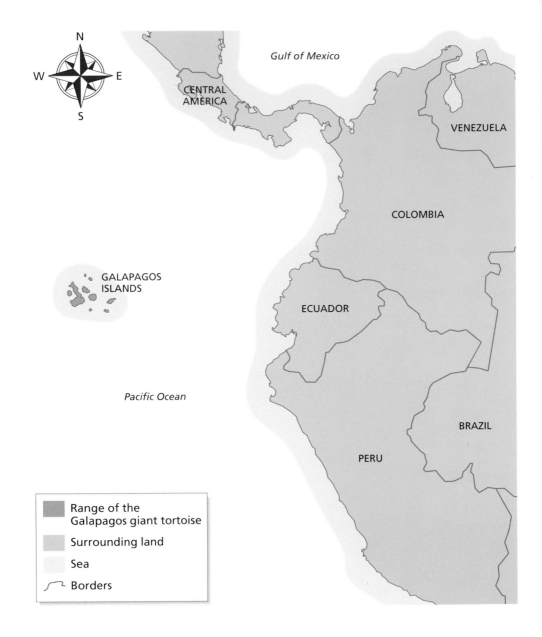

N
W   E
S

Gulf of Mexico

CENTRAL
AMERICA

VENEZUELA

COLOMBIA

GALAPAGOS
ISLANDS

ECUADOR

Pacific Ocean

BRAZIL

PERU

Range of the
Galapagos giant tortoise

Surrounding land

Sea

Borders

A quick look at tortoises

What do tortoises look like?

Tortoises have tough skin that covers their legs and head. The rest of their body is inside a hard shell. Most tortoises are coloured dull brown, grey, green or yellow. Some tortoises have bright coloured shells and skin.

Where do tortoises live?

Tortoises live all over the world, except very cold places like Antarctica. Many tortoises live in Africa and Madagascar. The largest tortoises in the world live on the Galapagos Islands off the coast of Ecuador.

What do tortoises eat?

Most tortoises eat mainly plants. They eat leaves, plants, grass and fruit. Other tortoises eat insects, snails and meat from dead animals that they find.

This Galapagos tortoise has its head
pulled inside its shell.

Tortoises in the rainforest

Tortoises are among the oldest **reptiles** on Earth. A reptile is a **cold-blooded** animal with a backbone. Cold-blooded animals have a body temperature that changes, depending on what the temperature is outside.

A tortoise is different from most reptiles because it has a shell. This hard outer covering protects its body. The shell is made up of three parts: the top and bottom shell and the bridge. The bridge connects the top and bottom shell. Most of the tortoise's body fits inside the shell. The shell has one opening for the tortoise's head and front legs, and one for the back legs and tail.

Tortoises belong to a group whose scientific name is Testudines. This name comes from the Latin word 'testa', which means shell.

∧ Tortoises like these gopher tortoises need
to live in warm places.

Where do tortoises live?

Tortoises live in most warm areas of the world.
They would freeze in cold areas because they are
cold-blooded. Many tortoises live in rainforests
and fields in Africa and Madagascar. A rainforest
is a warm place where many types of trees and
plants grow close together, and lots of rain falls.

Some tortoises live on islands. Galapagos tortoises live in the wet highland forests and the drier areas of the Galapagos Islands. Because there is so much food to eat, the Galapagos tortoises that live in the highland areas grow much larger than those that do not.

The trees and plants in the rainforests help tortoises hide from **predators**. Predators are animals that hunt other animals and eat them. Snakes, rats, wild dogs, pigs, cats, birds and other animals will catch and eat tortoises.

Tortoises have an important role in the rainforest. They eat rainforest fruits and plants. Some of the seeds from these fruits and plants leave their bodies as waste. Waste is what the body does not use or need from food that has been eaten. As tortoises move through rainforests, they spread the seeds to new places. New plants grow from the seeds.

Tortoises also help other animals in the rainforest. Some tortoises will let birds land on their legs and necks. The birds eat insects that are on the tortoises' skin. Many of these insects are harmful to tortoises. But the insects are an important food for the birds.

How are tortoises different from other turtles?

Tortoises are turtles that live almost all of their lives on land. They go to water only to drink it, if they are thirsty. Other turtles live most of their lives in water. Tortoises often live longer than other turtles do.

The shape of their shells is different, too. Other turtles have a flat shell that helps them swim. Because they do not swim, many tortoises have a high shell shaped like half a ball.

The feet and legs of a tortoise are not like the legs of a turtle. Turtles have long, thin legs. They have webbed feet on the end of their legs like ducks do. This helps them swim easily. Tortoises have thick, short legs that help them move more easily on land. They do not have webbed feet. Instead, their feet are covered with hard, tough skin. The tough skin lets them walk over rough places without their feet getting hurt. Their toenails help them grip as they climb over rocks and logs.

You can see the high, rounded shell of this tortoise.

▲ This red-footed tortoise is one of the most colourful species of tortoise.

What do tortoises look like?

There are more than forty **species** of tortoise, and many of them look very much alike. A species is a group of animals or plants that share common features and are closely related to each other.

Each tortoise species has its own style of shell. Shells can be unusual shapes with bumps and curves. Some are very hard and feel like a rock. Others are much softer and feel like leather.

Shells can be different colours too. Most tortoises in the rainforest have green, brown or yellow shells. These colours help **camouflage** the tortoises. Camouflage is special colouring or patterns that help an animal blend in with its surroundings. The camouflage helps tortoises hide among the plants and trees of the rainforest.

The red-footed tortoise lives in the rainforests of South America. Unlike many tortoises, the red-footed tortoise is very brightly coloured. It has spots of bright red and yellow on the skin that covers its head and legs.

Tortoises use their shells to stay safe from predators. If a tortoise senses danger, it pulls its legs and head inside its shell. It sometimes uses its legs to cover its face when in danger too.

The size of the tortoise depends on the species. The speckled tortoise is the smallest. It rarely grows larger than about 9 centimetres. Galapagos tortoises are the largest tortoises. They can weigh more than 300 kilograms.

This Galapagos tortoise is drinking water from a puddle.

What tortoises eat

Many tortoises are **herbivores**. Herbivores eat only plants. The tortoises who live in the rainforest eat the leaves and fruits of plants and trees that grow there.

Some tortoises that live in the rainforest are **omnivores**. Omnivores are animals that eat both plants and animals. These rainforest tortoises eat snails, insects and worms. They may also eat the meat from dead animals they find.

Tortoises can find water to drink in many ways. They drink water from puddles on the rainforest floor or from streams and lakes. They also drink water from the leaves of plants that grow close to the ground. Their bodies also use the water from the moist food that they eat.

This tortoise is grazing on a special type of grass.

Finding and eating food

Some tortoise species, such as the red-footed and the leopard, are **grazers**. Grazers are always eating whatever they can find, usually grass and leaves that are on the ground. Other tortoise species, such as the Galapagos, are **browsers**. Browsers pick and choose what they eat. They usually have longer necks. They stretch their necks so they can reach leaves and fruits that grow on bushes and short trees.

Tortoises do not have teeth. They have sharp edges around their mouths called beaks. Meat-eating tortoises catch and cut up prey with their beaks. Herbivorous tortoises use their beaks to cut up plants.

Tortoises swallow their food whole. They use enzymes to **digest** the food in their stomachs. To digest means to break down food so the body can use it. Enzymes are liquids in the tortoises' stomachs that break down pieces of food.

Like all reptiles, it takes a long time for tortoises to turn their food into energy that their bodies can use. This means they do not have to eat as often as other animals do. Most tortoises eat several times a week. If no food is around, they can go without eating for longer periods of time.

Galapagos tortoises like to eat, but they do not need to eat much. They can also store a lot of water in their bodies. Scientists believe these tortoises can live up to one year without eating or drinking water.

These two males are about to fight with each other.

A tortoise's life cycle

Female and male tortoises usually do not live together. They gather together during the mating season. Some tortoises mate once a year. Others mate more often.

Tortoises mate only with other tortoises from their own species. They can tell other members of their species by the colour and shape of their shells. When a male finds a female, he bobs his head up and down or from side to side. He makes special noises. Each species makes its own kind of noise. Some sound like chickens clucking. Other noises sound like grunts or low growls.

During the mating season, male tortoises may fight one another for females. Some male tortoises fight by crashing their shells into one another. The winner knocks the other male over and then mates with the female.

Young tortoises

After mating, female tortoises look for good places to lay their eggs. They find a sunny place with loose, moist soil. If the location does not receive sunlight, the eggs will not hatch. Once they have found a place, females dig holes in the ground. They lay their eggs in the holes. The number of eggs a female lays depends on the species. Some females lay more than a hundred eggs. Some lay just one. A group of tortoise eggs is called a clutch.

After laying eggs in the holes, females bury the eggs loosely with soil. This helps keep the eggs warm. It also hides the eggs from predators. Birds and snakes may try to find and eat the eggs.

Most females leave the eggs soon after they lay them. Some females guard the eggs. They fight predators that might try to eat the eggs.

Young tortoises grow inside the eggs. They hatch several months after their mother has laid her eggs. The young tortoises break out of the eggshells using a horny tip on the end of their noses. Then, they dig their way above ground.

This tortoise is hatching from its egg.

Their mother is gone, and they need to know what to do to survive. There are many dangers waiting for them. Predators eat many newly hatched tortoises before they have a chance to grow up.

Most tortoises live to be more than ten or fifteen years old. Galapagos tortoises can live to be more than 100 years old.

This leopard tortoise is basking in the sun.

A tortoise's day

Most tortoises begin their day when the sun comes up. They crawl into the sunlight to warm themselves. Then they lie in the sun. This is called **basking**. Basking helps them to raise their body temperatures because they are cold-blooded. Warmer body temperatures help them digest their food. When there is no food, tortoises stay cool and inactive because this uses up less energy. This is how they can live so long without eating or drinking.

When they are warm, tortoises become more active. They then begin looking for food by walking across the rainforest floor.

By noon, it usually becomes hotter. Since they are cold-blooded, tortoises get hotter, too. Tortoises will die if they become too hot. So they move into the shade of plants and trees. Many tortoises sit in water or roll in wet mud to cool off. They also seem to enjoy being in the rain.

Tortoises need to stay warm at night, or they will lose the body heat they got from the sun. Some dig holes called **burrows**. They crawl inside their burrows to stay warm. Other tortoises move into a mud puddle to sleep for the night. The mud coats their bodies and helps them hold in heat.

If it becomes hot or dry, tortoises can **estivate**. Estivate means to spend the summer in a sleep-like state. When a tortoise is estivating, it usually crawls into its burrow and stays still. This helps it save energy so it does not need to eat or drink. It can estivate for months. The tortoise becomes active again when it rains or the weather cools.

These tortoises are keeping cool by lying in this mud puddle.

The future of tortoises

There were once hundreds of species of tortoise. Now, many species have become extinct. Extinct means there are no animals of that kind left alive in the wild.

Many giant tortoises became extinct because they were hunted and eaten as food. Sailors used to catch giant tortoises. They turned the tortoises upside down and stacked them on top of each other in their ships. The tortoises could live for up to a year like that, without eating or drinking. The sailors ate the tortoises for fresh meat when they got hungry during their trips.

Today, many tortoises are in danger of becoming extinct. People still hunt tortoises. They eat tortoise meat and make belts and boots out of tortoises' skin. Other people use the shells to make combs and spectacle frames.

▲ These children are learning about
Galapagos tortoises.

What will happen to tortoises?

To protect tortoises, new laws are being created
in many countries where tortoises live. It is
against the law to hunt or sell tortoises as pets
in these countries.

Some scientists take male and female tortoises
out of the wild. They bring them to zoos to

Tortoises do not sweat. The skin on their legs is covered with scales. These small, hard pieces of skin help tortoises keep water in their bodies.

breed them. Breeding means to keep animals and plants, to produce more of them. Scientists do this so there will be more tortoises in the future. The young tortoises are protected so they can grow up to mate.

Most tortoises born in captivity can't live in the rainforest. They will die because they do not know how to find food there. Scientists try to teach these tortoises how to find food and hide better in the rainforest. Then they release the tortoises back into the wild. This is called reintroduction to the wild.

People who try to save tortoises hope that breeding and reintroduction will lead to more wild tortoises in the future. Many people understand that tortoises are important to life in the rainforest. They must teach other people what they know. Then tortoises can live in the rainforests for a long time.

shell
see page 7

head
see page 7

legs
see page 10

Glossary

basking getting warm by lying under heat, especially the sun

burrow hole or tunnel in the ground where an animal lives

browser plant-eating animal that eats mainly leaves and shoots from trees and bushes

camouflage colours, shapes and patterns that make something blend in with its background

cold-blooded animals with body temperatures that change according to their surroundings

digest to break down food so the body can use it

estivate to rest in a sleep-like state

grazer plant-eating animal that eats mainly grass

herbivore animal that eats only plants

omnivore animal that eats both plants and animals

predator animal that hunts other animals to eat

reptile cold-blooded animal with a tough skin covered in scales

species group of animals or plants most closely related to each other

Internet sites

The Galapagos Tortoise
www.rainforest-alliance.org/
resources/species/tortoise.html

Tortoise Fact Sheet
www.kidsplanet.org/factsheets/tortoise.html

Useful address

World Wildlife Fund-UK
Panda House, Weyside Park
Godalming, Surrey, GU7 1XR

Books to read

Theodorou, R; Telford, C. *Amazing Journeys: Up a Rainforest Tree. Heinemann Library, Oxford, 1998*

Index